Sing-Song Sid

Sing-Song Sid
© 1999 Creative Teaching Press, Inc.
Written by Margaret Allen, Ph.D.
Illustrated by Tuko Fujisaki
Project Director: Luella Connelly
Editor: Joel Kupperstein
Art Director: Tom Cochrane

Published in the United States of America by:
Creative Teaching Press, Inc.
P.O. Box 6017
Cypress, CA 90630-0017

CTP 2909

Sid likes to sing.

He sings a song.

He sings and hums all day long.

Bing-Bong Bing-Bong

Sid sees a tree.
Sid makes up a song.

5

Bing-bong. Bing-bong.
Bing-a-bang-bong all day long.

6

Sid sees a man ringing a bell.
Sid makes up a song.

7

Ding-dong. Ding-dong.
Ding-a-dang-dong all day long.

8

Sid sees his mom buying things.
Sid makes up a song.

9

Pling-plong. Pling-plong.
Pling-a-plang-plong all day long.

Sid sees kids playing Ping-Pong.
Sing-Song Sid makes up a song.

Ping-pong. Ping-pong.
Ping-a-pang-pong all day long.

Sid, Sid, the sing-song kid.

Sing, Sid, sing your song.

Sing-Song Sid sings all day long.

BOOK 9: Sing-Song Sid

Focus Skills: -ing, -ong, -ang

Focus-Skill Words			Sight Words	Story Words
b**ing**	b**ong**	b**ang**	likes	buying
d**ing**	d**ong**	d**ang**	sees	playing
p**ing**	l**ong**	p**ang**	things	ringing
pl**ing**	pl**ong**	pl**ang**	your	tree
s**ing**	p**ong**			
s**ing**s	s**ong**			

Focus-Skill Words contain a new skill or sound introduced in this book.

Sight Words are among the most common words encountered in the English language (appearing in this book for the first time in the series).

Story Words appear for the first time in this book and are included to add flavor and interest to the story. They may or may not be decodable.

Interactive Reading Idea

After reading *Sing-Song Sid*, take a walk around the neighborhood or school. Have your young reader listen for noises like *Sing-Song Sid* did and create sounds for the actions he or she sees. Help the child use his or her knowledge of letters and sounds to write words for the sounds—just like *Sing-Song Sid* did! See if your young reader created *-ing*, *-ong*, or *-ang* words. If so, compare them to the words in the book.